King OF THE Tightrope

WHEN THE GREAT BLONDIN RULED NIAGARA

Written by
DONNA JANELL BOWMAN

Illustrated by
ADAM GUSTAVSON

PEACHTREE
ATLANTA

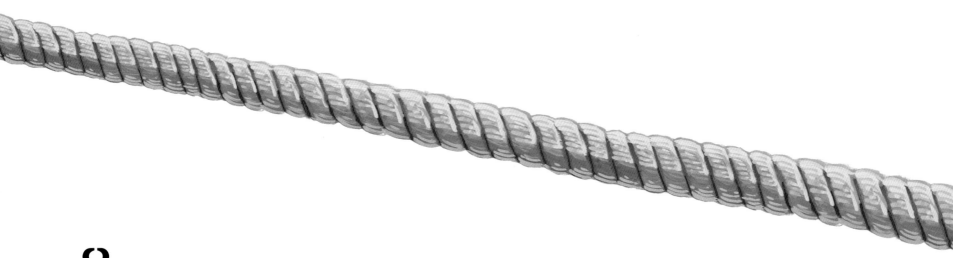

Published by
Peachtree Publishing Company Inc.
1700 Chattahoochee Avenue
Atlanta, Georgia 30318-2112
www.peachtree-online.com

Text © 2019 by Donna Janell Bowman
Illustrations © 2019 by Adam Gustavson

Edited by Kathy Landwehr
Design and composition by Nicola Simmonds Carmack
The illustrations for this book were created in gouache and watercolor on 140 lb. hot press watercolor paper.

Printed in March 2019 by Tien Wah Press in Malaysia
10 9 8 7 6 5 4 3 2 1
First Edition
ISBN 978-1-56145-937-7

Library of Congress Cataloging-in-Publication Data

Names: Bowman, Donna Janell, author. | Gustavson, Adam, illustrator.
Title: King of the tightrope : when the Great Blondin ruled Niagara / written by Donna Janell Bowman; illustrated by Adam Gustavson.
Description: First edition. | Atlanta : Peachtree Publishing Company Inc., [2019] | Audience: 006-010.
Identifiers: LCCN 2018010837 | ISBN 9781561459377
Subjects: LCSH: Blondin, 1824–1897–Juvenile literature. | Aerialists–France–Biography–Juvenile literature. | Niagara Falls (N.Y. and Ont.)–Juvenile literature.
Classification: LCC GV1811.B55 B69 2019 | DDC 796.46092 [B] –dc23 LC record available at *https://lccn.loc.gov/2018010837*

*To Justin,
who would have found a clever
way to engineer Blondin's rope.
And to Ethan, who would have
found a way to fish from it.
And to Jean-Louis Brenac, Blondin's
great-great-grandson, because his
French family has been missing from
Blondin's story for too long.*
—D. J. B.

For Freya. —A. G.

A rope-walker is like a poet, born and not made.

—Jean-François Gravelet

On a wintry day in 1859, a crowd gathered on the banks of Niagara Falls.

The wind blew.

The mist rose.

The falls roared.

People looked down and shivered at the crashing, thrashing waters below.

They envisioned falling, falling, falling!

But one feisty Frenchman looked up, up, up—
to the tip-top cliffs.

"What a splendid place to bridge with a tightrope,"
he said.

What kind of man has an idea like that?

That feisty Frenchman was born Jean-François Gravelet in 1824 in
a little town called Hesdin. His family members—all the way back to
grand-père Pierre—were acrobats, gymnasts, and funambulists. (That's
what tightrope walkers are called.)

They twirled, flipped, leaped, and skipped in circuses, theaters, and
carnival shows.

When Jean-François turned four, it was his turn to perform. But first
he had to learn to balance.

He toddled and wobbled along the edge of a thick board.

He fell. Again and again.

He soon learned to keep his shoulders straight and his knees *fléchis*.

He learned to keep his eyes ahead and his arms *ouverts*.

And he learned to keep his weight centered on the board for *équilibre!*

Then the thick board was replaced with thinner and thinner ones.

Finally, Jean-François was ready to learn about…

Corde—Rope!

There were ropes for lifting, towing, and anchoring. And, of course, ropes for walking on.

Jean-François watched riggers stretch, crank, clip, and clamp the ropes.

He learned the right knots, loops, hitches, and splices to secure them.

If the ropes weren't attached just so, the tightrope walker could tilt, teeter, and tumble. Jean-François didn't want that to happen to him.

Non!

Once he understood rigging, he practiced walking on a low rope.

As his rope was moved higher, he picked up a balance pole. It helped him keep his weight centered on the rope.

Soon, he was twirling, flipping, leaping, and skipping. He took to the rope like a spider takes to its web.

The Gravelet family troupe performed throughout France and beyond.

For *Mesdames et Messieurs* and for *les enfants*.

Even for royalty.

Audiences cheered loudest for Jean-François, "The Little Wonder."

Year after year, he climbed toward stardom.

Hourra! Magnifique!

It was *très bon* until…

Jean-François grew bored.
Performing on the rope had become too easy, too dull, too *ordinaire*.
Pff!
Surely if he could imagine more, he could do more.
So, he did.

He balanced on a teetering chair.
He somersaulted over flames.
He played musical instruments.
Fantastique!

In 1851, Jean-François was invited to perform in America. He knew just what to say.

Oui, s'il vous plaît!

He packed his tights, his buckskin slippers, and a new stage name—The Great Blondin.

During his long journey aboard the *Germania*, Blondin climbed the ship's masts.

He tied knots with sailors.

He practiced acrobatics on deck.

New ideas danced through his mind.

The Great Blondin's American tour was to last for two years. But those two years became four, then six, then more. His troupe zipped from America, to Cuba, to Canada.

His feats became more and more exciting—like carrying a man on his back or performing with his feet in baskets, or with chains wrapped around his body, or with a blindfold over his eyes.

It was *merveilleux* until, once again, it became too easy,
too dull, too *ordinaire*.
Pff!
Then, in 1858, he heard about…

Niagara Falls!

The Great Blondin traveled there, *tout de suite*.

He pictured a tightrope stretched between America's Goat Island
and Canada's Table Rock—straight over Horseshoe Falls.

Sensationnel!

He imagined it, but could he do it?

"To cross those roaring waters became the ambition of my life,"
Blondin later said.

In spring of 1859, Blondin and his agent, Harry Colcord, announced their plan to Niagara newspapers.

The reporters wrote about Blondin, calling him "insane," "damphule," and a "suicidal madman."

The skeptics wouldn't stop Blondin, but something else might…

The owners of Goat Island were so certain Blondin would fall to his death, they wouldn't allow him to attach his ropes to their land.

But downstream, the owners of White's Pleasure Grounds said yes.

Canadian officials on the opposite side of the river didn't object.

The spot was not directly over the falls, but at least Blondin could continue.

That is, *if* he could raise the money to pay for workers, equipment, and rope.

One day, Blondin paced the nearby
Railroad Suspension Bridge,
brainstorming ideas.
A stranger bet him that he couldn't
even walk down one of the thin
guy wires that stretched to the shore.
Blondin looked at the man.
He shrugged.

Then he jumped onto the wire and inched his way down toward the river's edge.

He stopped halfway across and swung by his feet.

Then he sashayed to the shore. And then up the wire to the bridge again.

Voilà!

Onlookers gasped.

Business owners and railroad managers saw dollar signs. They offered to pay Blondin's expenses.

Finally, the funambulist could get to work.

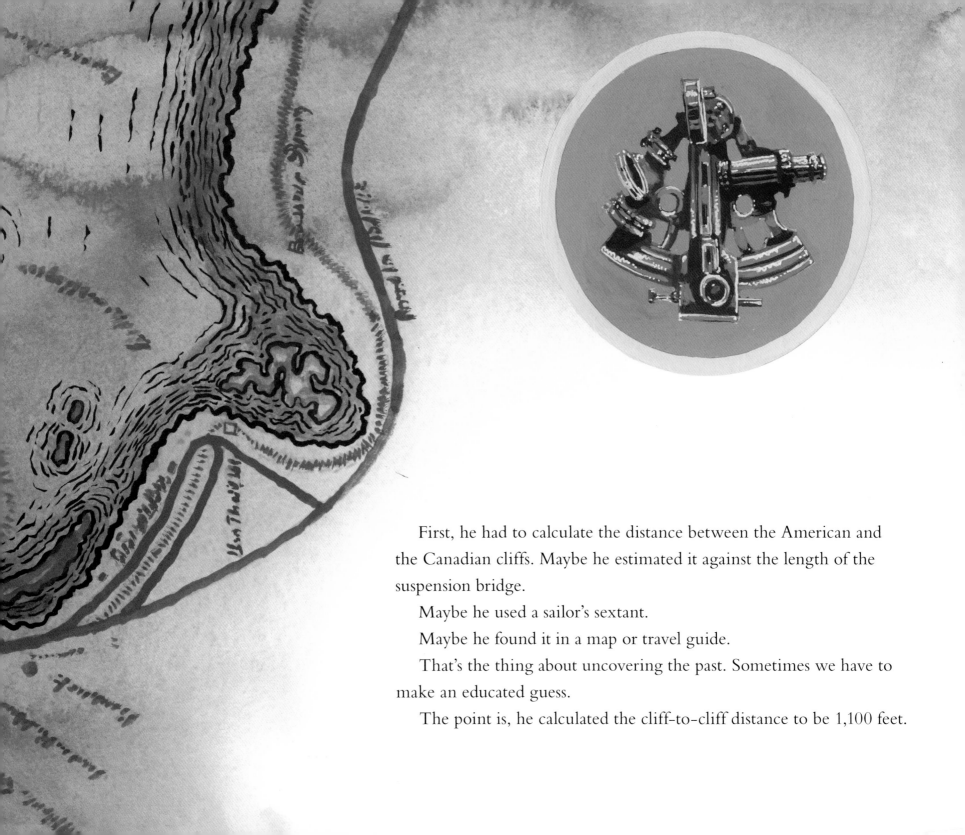

First, he had to calculate the distance between the American and the Canadian cliffs. Maybe he estimated it against the length of the suspension bridge.

Maybe he used a sailor's sextant.

Maybe he found it in a map or travel guide.

That's the thing about uncovering the past. Sometimes we have to make an educated guess.

The point is, he calculated the cliff-to-cliff distance to be 1,100 feet.

Blondin ordered 1,300 feet (396 meters) of hemp rope, 3.25 inches (8 centimeters) in diameter, more than ten inches in circumference. That's about as thick as a man's ankle. This would be the rope on which he would walk.

But how would he get the big walking rope across the river?

How would he attach it on each side, tighten it, and keep it steady?

How would he keep himself balanced in the windy space above the Niagara Gorge?

Blondin considered the challenges and researched his options.

At his request, a local merchant ordered 40,000 feet of smaller ropes and thin lines. He would use these for towing, anchoring, lifting, and steadying the walking rope.

On June 22, 1859, the walking rope arrived by train. It was so big that it had to be delivered in two sections.

The mountain of rope was loaded into a wagon and paraded through Niagara Falls Village.

People lined the streets, watching in disbelief.

They called Blondin a madman and a buffoon.

Newspapers declared his proposal a "fearful and foolish trick."

"Arrangements (for his funeral) are actively going on," wrote one reporter.

Blondin paid no attention. He spliced the two rope sections into one. Then he got ready with a step-by-step plan.

On the Canadian cliff, a special winch called a windlass was erected.

Far upstream on the American shore, men tied one end of a long towline to a tree. They rowed the rest of the towline across the raging river in a boat. The line broke. They started over.

Finally, the towline made it to Canada. Men attached it to the windlass and pushed the crank around and around, pulling the line across the gorge.

On the American side, the first towline was attached to a thicker towline. It, too, was pulled across the Niagara Gorge by the windlass.

Once that thicker towline was in place, the giant walking rope was tied to its end on the American side.

The men at the windlass heaved and strained.

The walking rope inched across the Niagara Gorge toward Canada.

One hundred feet.

Five hundred feet.

Eight hundred feet.

Arrêtez! Stop!

The walking rope was too heavy. The towline threatened to break. And if that happened, the walking rope would plunge into the river.

Blondin imagined a solution.

He tied another rope around his waist.

Men held the other end and slowly gave him slack.

He eased out onto the towline and over the river.

On shore, onlookers held their breath.

The towline swayed.

The walking rope swayed.

Blondin swayed.

If the towline broke now, he would
be slammed against the rocky cliff.

At last, Blondin tied his knots, checked them twice, and shimmied down to a tree at the water's edge.

A few more turns at the windlass was all the men could manage. The tension endangered the walking rope. But there was still a sixty-foot sag in the center.

For his safety, Blondin had to control the rope's sway.

He rigged a wheeled basket under the walking rope, loaded it with supplies, then climbed in himself. Helpers on the cliffs pulled him across the river.

He stopped about every eighteen feet, to loop, tie, and clip a guy line to the walking rope. The other ends of the guy lines were tied to trees and rocks at the water's edge.

Blondin marveled at the spider web of ropes across the Niagara Gorge. And at the swaying space in the center where guy lines couldn't reach.

Dangereux!

On June 30, 1859, thousands of people arrived by train, carriage, boat, and horseback.

Most came to cheer Blondin on.

Some hoped to see him fall.

Gamblers huddled in dark corners, placing bets against his life.

Wasn't Blondin afraid of falling, people asked him?

"There be one American Falls and one Canada Falls," he joked. "When Blondin Falls, there be one French Falls."

At 5:00 p.m., a cannon was fired. Show time!

Blondin climbed onto the platform and teased the crowd: "Gentlemen, anyone what please to cross, I carry him on my back."

Nobody volunteered.

Blondin stepped onto the walking rope.

He kept his shoulders straight and his knees *fléchis*.

He kept his eyes ahead and his arms *ouverts*.

Behind him, someone yelled, "Leave us a lock of your hair to remember you by."

Blondin barely noticed. He "marched on at a lively pace, his toes hardly appearing to touch the rope," a witness wrote.

Suddenly, a gust of wind slammed into him.

He whipped his balance pole left and right to steady himself.

Cheers turned to gasps. Would he make it?

To the crowd's relief, Blondin righted himself and struck a dancer's pose. Then he sat on the rope, as easily as if it was a chair.

There was nothing easy, dull, or *ordinaire* about it.

A moment later, he was on his feet trotting down toward *le milieu de la corde*—the middle of the rope.

There, he lay down on the rope—half of his body in America and half in Canada.

On shore, children hid behind their mothers' parasols.

Gentlemen shielded their eyes.

A few ladies fainted.

But Blondin was not afraid.

He had already done something *extrordinaire*— exactly as he had imagined.

Far below, the *Maid of the Mist* arrived. Blondin lowered a cord
to the boat, and the captain fastened a bottle of bubbly to the end.
Blondin pulled it back up and saluted to both shores.

Then he stood and traipsed uphill along his rope until he stepped
onto the Canadian cliff.

"My frens," he said to the waiting crowd, "I have got safely over.
I hope you will remember me."

Half an hour later, Blondin stepped back onto the rope and bid farewell to Canada.

On both shores, bands played, people cheered, and train whistles blew.

When he reached America, gentlemen lifted Blondin onto their shoulders and carried him through the village.

"You are as great as the Falls themselves!" somebody shouted.

"You can see that I am even greater!" Blondin replied.

Newspaper reporters changed their stories.

"The Great Feat has been Successfully Performed!"

"It is useless: you cannot describe Blondin, any more than you can describe Niagara; both are stupendous and baffling."

"In utter amazement we inquire, what will Blondin do next?"

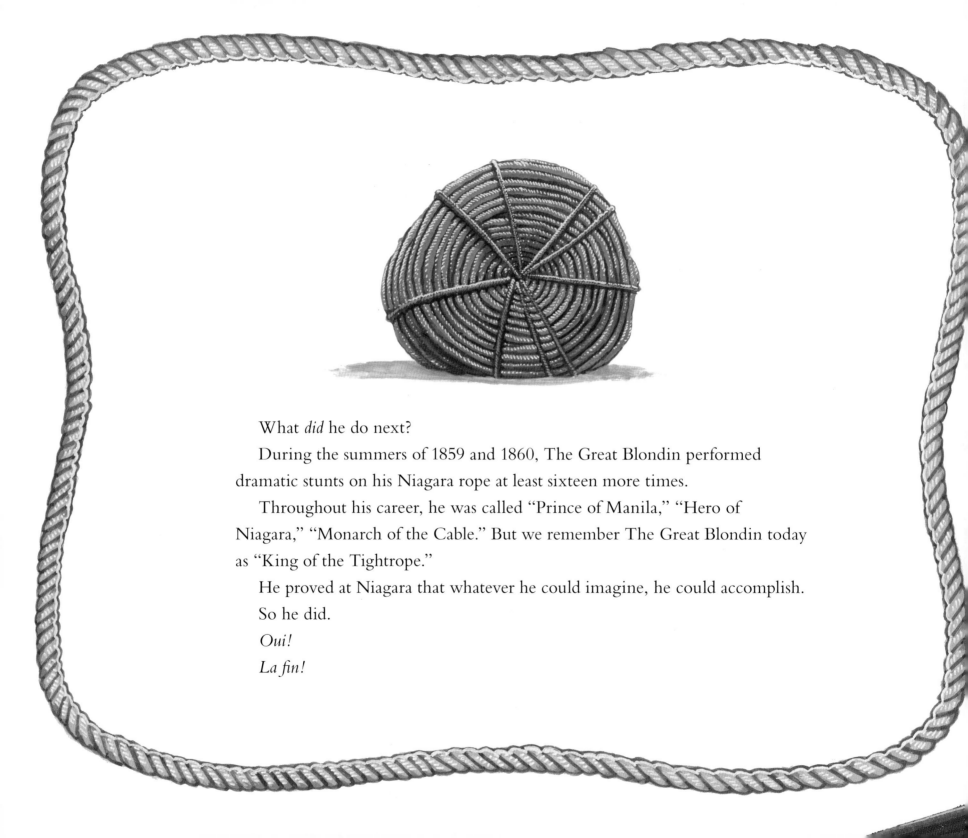

What *did* he do next?

During the summers of 1859 and 1860, The Great Blondin performed dramatic stunts on his Niagara rope at least sixteen more times.

Throughout his career, he was called "Prince of Manila," "Hero of Niagara," "Monarch of the Cable." But we remember The Great Blondin today as "King of the Tightrope."

He proved at Niagara that whatever he could imagine, he could accomplish. So he did.

Oui!

La fin!

Merveilleux Moments!

1824
Born in Hesdin, France

1825
Makes his first public appearance at the coronation of Charles X of France, where his father pushes him in a wheelbarrow on a tightrope

1828
Climbs a slant rope to comfort his sister during a performance

1832
Performs for the King of Sardinia

1851
Travels to America on the *Germania* to perform with the Gabriel Ravel Troupe

Fantastique Facts!

- Blondin was 5 feet 6 inches (1.7 meters) tall and weighed about 145 pounds (66 kilograms).

- His stage name was inspired by his blond hair.

- Thirty years after the Niagara feats, a reporter claimed that Blondin had stood on his head on the rope so often, a ridge formed in his skull.

- According to Blondin, his most difficult feat was balancing on a chair and his most dangerous was riding a bicycle on the rope, which he introduced in 1868.

1851–1858
Performs with three troupes, as well as his own circus

June 30, 1859
Crosses the Niagara River on a tightrope for the first time

1859–1860
Performs stunts on his Niagara rope at least sixteen more times

1861
Sails to England aboard the *Bremen* to perform at London's Crystal Palace. Buys a home in England, which he names Niagara Villa

1861–1896
Travels the world, performing on the tightrope

1897
Dies from complications of diabetes

Dangereux Deeds!

- A wheelbarrow was often part of Blondin's act. At various times, he pushed a live lion, his children, or fireworks on the rope. One time, fireworks caught his clothes on fire.

- He performed at night with Bengal lights (a kind of fireworks) attached to the ends of his balance pole. Part way across, they fell into the Niagara River, leaving him to walk in darkness.

- In one of his other performances at Niagara, he walked on stilts on the rope. The Prince of Wales was in the audience.

- He walked a tightrope stretched between the masts of a ship.

- He carried a stove onto the rope, which he used to cook an omelet.

Magnifique Measurements!

Blondin's first towline was 2,300 feet (701 meters) long and a half inch (1.27 centimeters) in diameter.

The second towline was 7/8 inches (2 centimeters) in diameter.

His walking rope was 3.25 inches (8.25 centimeters) in diameter.

Blondin determined the circumference of his ropes by multiplying diameter times π(3.14159).

381—Blondin's Rope Ascension over Niagara River.

Sensationnel Statistics!

THIS SPACE FOR WRITING MESSAGES

POST CARD

PLA STAMP
DOME ONE
FOR TWO

THIS SPACE FOR ADDRESS

Niagara Falls was formed at least 12,000 years ago.

Niagara Falls divides the United States and Canada.

The Falls is actually composed of three separate waterfalls: Horseshoe, Bridal Veil, and American.

In 1859, Blondin's rope was stretched about 175 feet (53 meters) above the water on the Canadian side and about 165 (50 meters) on the American side.

Four out of the five Great Lakes (Superior, Michigan, Huron, Erie) drain into the Niagara River, which feeds the Falls.

Today, up to 750,000 gallons (34,096 hectoliters) of water flow over the Falls per second.

In 1859, the flow was almost 1,500,000 gallons (68,191 hectoliters) per sec

Balancing the Facts

In 2010, I learned about The Great Blondin from a PBS television program about Niagara Falls. I had to learn the how and why behind his spectacular endeavors, especially his Niagara feats. After a twisty, complex research journey, I realized Blondin was an artist called to create and inspire, though his chosen stage was a thread high above the ground—or should I say river. A perfect example of art meeting science, Blondin, like all ropewalkers, employed engineering and physics concepts to facilitate his art. Ultimately, the indomitable spirit of Jean-François Gravelet, The Great Blondin, reminds us that success begins where imagination meets determination.

To research The Great Blondin

- I bought manila ropes so that I could feel them under my feet.
- I read countless newspaper accounts. Many contain conflicting or missing details about Blondin's ropes, balance pole, and Niagara process.
- I discovered that the first Blondin biography, published in 1862, contained fictional elements, which have been perpetuated in later writings.
- To deconstruct Blondin's Niagara process, my son Justin's engineering education proved helpful. But, the invaluable input from Jean-Louis Brenac, Blondin's French great-great-grandson, also an engineer, brought Blondin's process and his French family into focus.

For bibliography, quotation sources, and extended content, see *www.donnajanellbowman.com*